A HIGHER YOU

VIBE SHOP

Congratulations, you've made an important investment in a therapy session that leaves you feeling free and your pockets full!

Step 1. Light any candle and set an intention

Example: Please help me release the anger I feel surrounding *insert event here*

Step 2. Write down whatever is troubling you, and why. (Be detailed)

Step 3. Rip those pages from this book. You don't need that energy anymore!

Step 4. Set the pages ablaze. Burn Baby Burn! (safely of course)

As the pages burn feel yourself releasing that heavy energy

Step 5. Give gratitude for the support in manifesting your intention

Step 6. Turn on your favorite song and dance in celebration!!!

ahigheryouvs.com

TODAY I RELEASE

DATE:

"FEELING GOOD IS A CHOICE."

TODAY I RELEASE

DATE:

"FEELING GOOD IS A CHOICE."

TODAY I RELEASE

DATE:

"FEELING GOOD IS A CHOICE."

TODAY I RELEASE

DATE:

"FEELING GOOD IS A CHOICE."

TODAY I RELEASE

DATE:

"FEELING GOOD IS A CHOICE."

TODAY I RELEASE

DATE:

"FEELING GOOD IS A CHOICE."

TODAY I RELEASE

DATE:

"FEELING GOOD IS A CHOICE."

TODAY I RELEASE

DATE:

"FEELING GOOD IS A CHOICE."

TODAY I RELEASE

DATE:

"FEELING GOOD IS A CHOICE."

TODAY I RELEASE

DATE:

"FEELING GOOD IS A CHOICE."

TODAY I RELEASE

DATE:

"FEELING GOOD IS A CHOICE."

TODAY I RELEASE

DATE:

"FEELING GOOD IS A CHOICE."

TODAY I RELEASE

DATE:

"FEELING GOOD IS A CHOICE."

TODAY I RELEASE

DATE:

"FEELING GOOD IS A CHOICE."

TODAY I RELEASE

DATE:

"FEELING GOOD IS A CHOICE."

TODAY I RELEASE

DATE:

"FEELING GOOD IS A CHOICE."

TODAY I RELEASE

DATE:

"FEELING GOOD IS A CHOICE."

TODAY I RELEASE

DATE:

"FEELING GOOD IS A CHOICE."

TODAY I RELEASE

DATE:

"FEELING GOOD IS A CHOICE."

TODAY I RELEASE

DATE:

"FEELING GOOD IS A CHOICE."

TODAY I RELEASE

DATE:

"FEELING GOOD IS A CHOICE."

TODAY I RELEASE

DATE:

"FEELING GOOD IS A CHOICE."

TODAY I RELEASE

DATE:

"FEELING GOOD IS A CHOICE."

TODAY I RELEASE

DATE:

"FEELING GOOD IS A CHOICE."

TODAY I RELEASE

DATE:

"FEELING GOOD IS A CHOICE."

TODAY I RELEASE

DATE:

"FEELING GOOD IS A CHOICE."

TODAY I RELEASE

DATE:

"FEELING GOOD IS A CHOICE."

TODAY I RELEASE

DATE:

"FEELING GOOD IS A CHOICE."

TODAY I RELEASE

DATE:

"FEELING GOOD IS A CHOICE."

TODAY I RELEASE

DATE:

"FEELING GOOD IS A CHOICE."

TODAY I RELEASE

DATE:

"FEELING GOOD IS A CHOICE."

TODAY I RELEASE

DATE:

"FEELING GOOD IS A CHOICE."

TODAY I RELEASE

DATE:

"FEELING GOOD IS A CHOICE."

TODAY I RELEASE

DATE:

"FEELING GOOD IS A CHOICE."

TODAY I RELEASE

DATE:

"FEELING GOOD IS A CHOICE."

TODAY I RELEASE

DATE:

"FEELING GOOD IS A CHOICE."

TODAY I RELEASE

DATE:

"FEELING GOOD IS A CHOICE."

TODAY I RELEASE

DATE:

"FEELING GOOD IS A CHOICE."

TODAY I RELEASE

DATE:

"FEELING GOOD IS A CHOICE."

TODAY I RELEASE

DATE:

"FEELING GOOD IS A CHOICE."

TODAY I RELEASE

DATE:

"FEELING GOOD IS A CHOICE."

TODAY I RELEASE

DATE:

"FEELING GOOD IS A CHOICE."

TODAY I RELEASE

DATE:

"FEELING GOOD IS A CHOICE."

TODAY I RELEASE

DATE:

"FEELING GOOD IS A CHOICE."

TODAY I RELEASE

DATE:

"FEELING GOOD IS A CHOICE."

TODAY I RELEASE

DATE:

"FEELING GOOD IS A CHOICE."

TODAY I RELEASE

DATE:

"FEELING GOOD IS A CHOICE."

TODAY I RELEASE

DATE:

"FEELING GOOD IS A CHOICE."

TODAY I RELEASE

DATE:

"FEELING GOOD IS A CHOICE."

TODAY I RELEASE

DATE:

"FEELING GOOD IS A CHOICE."

TODAY I RELEASE

DATE:

"FEELING GOOD IS A CHOICE."

TODAY I RELEASE

DATE:

"FEELING GOOD IS A CHOICE."

TODAY I RELEASE

DATE:

"FEELING GOOD IS A CHOICE."

TODAY I RELEASE

DATE:

"FEELING GOOD IS A CHOICE."

TODAY I RELEASE

DATE:

"FEELING GOOD IS A CHOICE."

TODAY I RELEASE

DATE:

"FEELING GOOD IS A CHOICE."

TODAY I RELEASE

DATE:

"FEELING GOOD IS A CHOICE."

TODAY I RELEASE

DATE:

"FEELING GOOD IS A CHOICE."

TODAY I RELEASE

DATE:

"FEELING GOOD IS A CHOICE."

TODAY I RELEASE

DATE:

"FEELING GOOD IS A CHOICE."

TODAY I RELEASE

DATE:

"FEELING GOOD IS A CHOICE."

TODAY I RELEASE

DATE:

"FEELING GOOD IS A CHOICE."

TODAY I RELEASE

DATE:

"FEELING GOOD IS A CHOICE."

TODAY I RELEASE

DATE:

"FEELING GOOD IS A CHOICE."

TODAY I RELEASE

DATE:

"FEELING GOOD IS A CHOICE."

TODAY I RELEASE

DATE:

"FEELING GOOD IS A CHOICE."

TODAY I RELEASE

DATE:

"FEELING GOOD IS A CHOICE."

TODAY I RELEASE

DATE:

"FEELING GOOD IS A CHOICE."

TODAY I RELEASE

DATE:

"FEELING GOOD IS A CHOICE."

TODAY I RELEASE

DATE:

"FEELING GOOD IS A CHOICE."

TODAY I RELEASE

DATE:

"FEELING GOOD IS A CHOICE."

TODAY I RELEASE

DATE:

"FEELING GOOD IS A CHOICE."

TODAY I RELEASE

DATE:

"FEELING GOOD IS A CHOICE."

TODAY I RELEASE

DATE:

"FEELING GOOD IS A CHOICE."

TODAY I RELEASE

DATE:

"FEELING GOOD IS A CHOICE."

TODAY I RELEASE

DATE:

"FEELING GOOD IS A CHOICE."

TODAY I RELEASE

DATE:

"FEELING GOOD IS A CHOICE."

TODAY I RELEASE

DATE:

"FEELING GOOD IS A CHOICE."

TODAY I RELEASE

DATE:

"FEELING GOOD IS A CHOICE."

TODAY I RELEASE

DATE:

"FEELING GOOD IS A CHOICE."

TODAY I RELEASE

DATE:

"FEELING GOOD IS A CHOICE."

TODAY I RELEASE

DATE:

"FEELING GOOD IS A CHOICE."

TODAY I RELEASE

DATE:

"FEELING GOOD IS A CHOICE."

TODAY I RELEASE

DATE:

"FEELING GOOD IS A CHOICE."

TODAY I RELEASE

DATE:

"FEELING GOOD IS A CHOICE."

TODAY I RELEASE

DATE:

"FEELING GOOD IS A CHOICE."

TODAY I RELEASE

DATE:

"FEELING GOOD IS A CHOICE."

TODAY I RELEASE

DATE:

"FEELING GOOD IS A CHOICE."

TODAY I RELEASE

DATE:

"FEELING GOOD IS A CHOICE."

TODAY I RELEASE

DATE:

"FEELING GOOD IS A CHOICE."

TODAY I RELEASE

DATE:

"FEELING GOOD IS A CHOICE."

TODAY I RELEASE

DATE:

"FEELING GOOD IS A CHOICE."

TODAY I RELEASE

DATE:

"FEELING GOOD IS A CHOICE."

TODAY I RELEASE

DATE:

"FEELING GOOD IS A CHOICE."

TODAY I RELEASE

DATE:

"FEELING GOOD IS A CHOICE."

TODAY I RELEASE

DATE:

"FEELING GOOD IS A CHOICE."

TODAY I RELEASE

DATE:

"FEELING GOOD IS A CHOICE."

TODAY I RELEASE

DATE:

"FEELING GOOD IS A CHOICE."

TODAY I RELEASE

DATE:

"FEELING GOOD IS A CHOICE."

TODAY I RELEASE

DATE:

"FEELING GOOD IS A CHOICE."

TODAY I RELEASE

DATE:

"FEELING GOOD IS A CHOICE."

TODAY I RELEASE

DATE:

"FEELING GOOD IS A CHOICE."

TODAY I RELEASE

DATE:

"FEELING GOOD IS A CHOICE."

TODAY I RELEASE

DATE:

"FEELING GOOD IS A CHOICE."

TODAY I RELEASE

DATE:

"FEELING GOOD IS A CHOICE."

TODAY I RELEASE

DATE:

"FEELING GOOD IS A CHOICE."

TODAY I RELEASE

DATE:

"FEELING GOOD IS A CHOICE."

TODAY I RELEASE

DATE:

"FEELING GOOD IS A CHOICE."

TODAY I RELEASE

DATE:

"FEELING GOOD IS A CHOICE."

TODAY I RELEASE

DATE:

"FEELING GOOD IS A CHOICE."

TODAY I RELEASE

DATE:

"FEELING GOOD IS A CHOICE."

TODAY I RELEASE

DATE:

"FEELING GOOD IS A CHOICE."

TODAY I RELEASE

DATE:

"FEELING GOOD IS A CHOICE."

TODAY I RELEASE

DATE:

"FEELING GOOD IS A CHOICE."

TODAY I RELEASE

DATE:

"FEELING GOOD IS A CHOICE."

TODAY I RELEASE

DATE:

"FEELING GOOD IS A CHOICE."

TODAY I RELEASE

DATE:

"FEELING GOOD IS A CHOICE."

TODAY I RELEASE

DATE:

"FEELING GOOD IS A CHOICE."

TODAY I RELEASE

DATE:

"FEELING GOOD IS A CHOICE."

TODAY I RELEASE

DATE:

"FEELING GOOD IS A CHOICE."

TODAY I RELEASE

DATE:

"FEELING GOOD IS A CHOICE."

TODAY I RELEASE

DATE:

"FEELING GOOD IS A CHOICE."

TODAY I RELEASE

DATE:

"FEELING GOOD IS A CHOICE."

TODAY I RELEASE

DATE:

"FEELING GOOD IS A CHOICE."

TODAY I RELEASE

DATE:

"FEELING GOOD IS A CHOICE."

TODAY I RELEASE

DATE:

"FEELING GOOD IS A CHOICE."

TODAY I RELEASE

DATE:

"FEELING GOOD IS A CHOICE."

TODAY I RELEASE

DATE:

"FEELING GOOD IS A CHOICE."

TODAY I RELEASE

DATE:

"FEELING GOOD IS A CHOICE."

TODAY I RELEASE

DATE:

"FEELING GOOD IS A CHOICE."

TODAY I RELEASE

DATE:

"FEELING GOOD IS A CHOICE."

TODAY I RELEASE

DATE:

"FEELING GOOD IS A CHOICE."

TODAY I RELEASE

DATE:

"FEELING GOOD IS A CHOICE."

TODAY I RELEASE

DATE:

"FEELING GOOD IS A CHOICE."

TODAY I RELEASE

DATE:

"FEELING GOOD IS A CHOICE."

TODAY I RELEASE

DATE:

"FEELING GOOD IS A CHOICE."

TODAY I RELEASE

DATE:

"FEELING GOOD IS A CHOICE."

TODAY I RELEASE

DATE:

"FEELING GOOD IS A CHOICE."

TODAY I RELEASE

DATE:

"FEELING GOOD IS A CHOICE."

TODAY I RELEASE

DATE:

"FEELING GOOD IS A CHOICE."

TODAY I RELEASE

DATE:

"FEELING GOOD IS A CHOICE."

TODAY I RELEASE

DATE:

"FEELING GOOD IS A CHOICE."

TODAY I RELEASE

DATE:

"FEELING GOOD IS A CHOICE."

TODAY I RELEASE

DATE:

"FEELING GOOD IS A CHOICE."

TODAY I RELEASE

DATE:

"FEELING GOOD IS A CHOICE."

TODAY I RELEASE

DATE:

"FEELING GOOD IS A CHOICE."

TODAY I RELEASE

DATE:

"FEELING GOOD IS A CHOICE."

Made in the USA
Middletown, DE
07 October 2022

12239206R00084